# Growth in Prayer

## Jim Wilson

James Clarke & Co
Cambridge

First published 1964
Reprinted 1982

ISBN 0 227 67475 8

© The Guild of Health 1964


Published by
James Clarke & Co
7 All Saints' Passage
Cambridge
CB2 3LS
England

Printed and bound in Great Britain by
Redwood Burn Limited, Trowbridge, Wiltshire

# CONTENTS

## PART I

## PART II

# PREFACE

My first book, *First Steps in Meditation for Young People*, brought many requests for second steps. This book is intended to provide a meditation for every day in the year. The meditation given for the Sunday should be used every day for the whole week. Some will be able to repeat the sentence given, over and over in the mind for five minutes, others for ten or fifteen minutes. A group of people could meet, even if only two or three, each week for twenty minutes to use this book. One of them would read the passage from the Bible and then say the prayer. A short silence would then follow. Then the instruction would be read or could be expanded by the leader of the group. Then there would be silence for the meditation, followed by thanksgiving. May God bless all those who thus seek a deeper knowledge of Him and of His purposes for them and for the world!

JIM WILSON

THE GUILD OF HEALTH,
EDWARD WILSON HOUSE,
26, QUEEN ANNE STREET,
LONDON, W.1.

# GROWTH IN PRAYER

## I  KNOWING GOD

Our whole prayer life depends on what we believe deeply in our mind about God. Wrong, or unworthy ideas about God will lead to disappointment and ineffectiveness in prayer; and yet belief about God is not enough. We need to know God in our experience, and deep prayer is needed if we are to know Him in this way.

"No man hath seen God at any time," and we can only know the truth about Him as it has been shown to us in the Old Testament revelation and in Jesus Christ and through the Creation which has been made by Him. But if we learn to wait on Him in prayer and meditation we begin to experience His Spirit working in our own lives and influencing us. Then we begin to know Him, which is much more than knowing about Him. As we begin to experience His Peace, His Love, His Joy and His fulness of Life, we know beyond all doubt that God is real. But this can only come through persevering prayer and meditation. What do we believe about God? This is not a theological book but we can put it simply.

Jesus taught us to say "Our Father" and He spoke of "My Father and your Father" and He thought of God's life "in all" the world and of us "in Him," and of Himself "in us." St. Paul speaks of God as "The Father, who is above all and through all and in you all." "It is in Him that we live and move and have our being for we also are His offspring."

God then is creative Spirit and His presence fills both heaven and earth. You can't picture that. His spirit is far bigger than all creation and is also in every part of it—"above all and through all" and therefore "in you all." So, every single person in all the world lives in God and

5

God's creative Spirit is within him or her. And because His Spirit is creative it is working to express itself, and it does so in the flowers and in everything that is good and perfect in all creation, though a large part of creation has " missed the mark " and has "fallen short of " expressing the glory of God : it is a fallen creation and there is much evil in it, but God works in it all to overcome evil and to perfect it. " My Father worketh hitherto and I work," said Jesus. So we believe that God's life and spirit is always in us waiting to be released into expression in us, but can only do so when we respond and believe in Him and wait on Him in prayer. When His life and Spirit begins to express itself in a deep sense of calmness and a deeper love in our human relationships, or a deeper sense of joy in life, we are beginning to know God. Then, knowing Him and His good purposes for men and for creation, we want to be united with Him and to help Him.


## II  UNDERSTANDING OURSELVES

It is important, if we are to pray effectively, that we should know something about ourselves and particularly about our mind and how it works. Our human nature is made to express God. We are intended to grow into and to become true sons and daughters of God, reflecting His character.

Our human nature is a trinity in unity consisting of spirit, soul and body (1 Thess. $5^{23}$), and we also have a mind which functions, partly through the physical body and partly through the soul. The mind is also a trinity in unity. The conscious, the subconscious and the unconscious mind are not three minds but one. We think with the conscious mind, and we can only normally think of one thing at a time. If we are making toast and we begin to think of something else the toast goes out of our mind and it burns.

The subconscious mind holds many memories which we

can recover easily. You can remember what you did on your holiday last year.

The unconscious mind holds many memories which we are not able "to bring to mind" at all. Some may be happy, others are the reverse. We have a tendency to repress unhappy or unpleasant memories and to push them down into the unconscious mind, and with them goes all the emotion which was originally stirred by the event. Thus we have much misery and fear and sometimes resentment or anxiety buried in our unconscious minds. In later life this sediment of unhappy and perhaps negative, and it may be even unbelieving feeling, tends to push up into consciousness and becomes the underlying cause of unhappiness or fear and other feelings, which we do not understand, and often causes illness or even disease.

Our physical healing often depends on the healing of our deep unconscious mind and its affect on our souls. We need the redemptive power of Christ for our whole person and this includes the mind, soul, and body. " Be ye transformed by the renewing of your mind " (Romans $12^2$).

This healing can be greatly helped by prayer and meditation; and by this deep healing both our characters and our body can often be healed and we then glorify God by growing more like Him, becoming true sons of God. We are made by God to reflect His own wholeness as well as His Holiness. Calmness and peace of heart and a love which refrains from unkind criticism and looks for good in others, and a happy outlook on life are quite as much a part of wholeness as health of body.

LET THIS MIND BE IN YOU WHICH WAS ALSO IN CHRIST JESUS.


## III  GROWTH IN PRAYER

Just as there is development in a child's way of talking and powers of conversation, and as our means of communication with others change as we grow up, so ought our methods of prayer to change and develop as we learn to know God more truly.

(1) PRAYER OF PETITION. We are generally taught as children to ask our Father for things which we need. This is as natural as a child asking his father on earth; but a child who badgers his father is a nuisance. Jesus taught us to ask as children : "Ask and it shall be given you, seek and ye shall find, knock and it shall be opened " (St. Matt. 7[7]). This is a first step, but children should be taught to thank God and to praise Him and to express their love to Him. There should be growth even in a small child's prayer, leading to less selfish prayer.

(2) UNSELFISH PETITION. The Lord's Prayer is a distinct advance in the growth of prayer. It has seven petitions and none of them is selfish. The disciples asked for teaching on prayer, and Jesus gave them a method of prayer : "After this manner pray ye " (Matt. 6[9]). It is a method based on our unity and brotherhood in our Father's family : it is concerned with our Father's purposes ("Thy Kingdom come, Thy will be done "). God's will and His Kingdom will not be achieved through individual efforts alone : it will come through the activity of many individuals, in the Community of the Church, each making his contribution, and each drawing strength from all the others in it. The Lord's Prayer, therefore, begins with personal relationships. As we say "Our " we ought to wait and think who we mean by "Our." It means more than "My " Father. Then, with all those whom we include in those words "Our Father," we become concerned in God's purposes for the world, and in our own needs only in the light of the needs of others.

The Lord's Prayer, if used in this way, will prepare us for the next step in prayer.

(3) LITURGICAL PRAYER. That is, forms of prayer which can be used by the Community of the Church in worship together. Some of these are very old, such as the Creeds,

the Gloria, the Sursum Corda in the Communion service. These, and some of the Collects and the more positive of the psalms and hymns can be learned by heart and will become part of our daily prayer, expressing praise and adoration to God. These will come naturally to our hearts in moments of thankfulness or need of God.

## IV   GROWTH IN PRAYER

Growth in prayer must never be thought of as going on from one method, which we then leave behind, to another. The more developed method, which we may move on to, enlightens and develops the earlier methods and so we find ourselves still, at different times, using all the earlier methods of prayer. We ask God for things we need more confidently because we have gone on to less selfish ways of prayer and thought. We ask now that we may be able " to ask such things as shall please Thee." Not asking so much that God will grant my petitions but that I may be able to fulfil His desires. Not asking God to do something which I want for some sick person, and possibly doubting if He will do so, but asking God to use me as His means of helping my sick friend. Thus we make God the centre of intercession, by taking the whole world and God's plan for every detail of it into our hearts where there is intense desire for God's Kingdom and such simple faith and loyalty to Christ that leaves no room for self. Not using God for our own ends but offering ourselves to be used by Him. But how can this come about? Only by finding time to be alone and to meditate.

(4) MEDITATION. The word " meditation " is applied to several methods of spiritual exercise, some more, some less intellectual, but all valuable. Most people begin with discursive meditation. In this we use our intellect and powers of thought in an endeavour to learn to know more about God, and by the light of the Holy Spirit to know Him

9

better. We take a passage of Scripture and read and dwell upon it thoughtfully. Our imagination pictures the scene : our feelings are stirred and perhaps our affection towards God is expressed in penitence or thanksgiving or love, and we end by using our will in making some resolution which arises out of the meditation.

If persevered with day by day this method of meditation will lead us to a deeper knowledge of God and to a fuller understanding of the Scriptures, but it has dangers. It may become merely Bible study and stop at that, and be so satisfying in that way to some people that it ceases to be a part of their prayer life leading on to closer fellowship with God. Meditation can also become a mere preparation for a Sunday School Class or a sermon. It ought not to be a means of thinking out what I am to say to others but of hearing what God will say to me by His Holy Spirit.

Faithful meditation of this kind will lead us to a deeper understanding of God and of His ways, but most of this will be upon the intellectual level and we still need a method which will bring us to a deeper experience of God Himself.


## V   GROWTH IN PRAYER

Most people never get past the four stages in the growth of Prayer which I have spoken of. They say their morning and evening prayers and go to church and find time to meditate, but it never gets very deep with them. This is a great loss to them because we ought, everyone of us, to go on to a much deeper knowledge and personal experience of the reality of God. We do this in the fifth step.

(5)   CONTEMPLATIVE MEDITATION. This is a step between Meditation and Contemplation. Contemplation is the final step in the growth of the prayer life in which we experience union with God such as our Lord spoke of in St. John 17. In Contemplative Meditation (which is sometimes called

" affective prayer ") we learn to wait on God and in quietness allow Him to make Himself known to us.

We sit, in a disciplined way, both feet flat on the ground, hands folded on the lap, back straight and head up. In this way we can become entirely relaxed physically and then in mind, letting all self-concern go into the care of God and letting all self-effort go, that God may be able to speak and teach us. We then repeat a short sentence, which is entirely based on God, expressing the truth. " Be still and know that I am peace within you," or " Lo I am with you always." We repeat the words over and over, and this helps to keep the mind from straying. It also helps to by-pass the conscious mind and to allow the truth to sink into the unconscious mind and into the soul. There it will begin to change what is dark and negative. It will bring about a healing by a change in our deep consciousness. This will, as we persevere, bring about changes in our character : we become more peaceful and calm and learn to have a deeper love which changes our personal relationships. As we persevere it has its effect on the body and we have a greater resistance to disease : we begin to experience what our Lord spoke of as " fullness of life." To begin with we only do this for three or four minutes each day : children will begin with much shorter times. We don't expect any results or any feelings while we are doing it. The proof of its value comes at length in a much deeper awareness of the reality of God and in our experience of His spirit guiding and changing us.

(6) CONTEMPLATION. If we persevere with Contemplative Meditation, we may find our souls being caught up into a deep union with God. This experience will be entirely unselfconscious. It is not achieved by any effort of our own. It is an experience which some will enter into only for a few seconds for it will be gone the moment we know that we have reached it, for we will then have become selfconscious. On the other hand, there are some people who may have

11

a vocation to such prayer, but it will not be to a mere enjoyment of God nor to a mere ecstatic adoration and love for Him, for God is the Creator of the Universe and He is in all as well as above all, and He purposes to overcome all evil by suffering and to bring His Kingdom into being on earth as it is in Heaven. Our union, therefore, will be with Him in all His purposes for Creation and in His Cross as well as in His glorified and risen life.


## VI GROWTH IN PRAYER

We have now thought of six stages in the development of the prayer life.

(a) The simple childlike petition—which is often selfish and treats God as if He was far away from us, in a rather demanding way.

(b) The prayer of relationships, which begins with the word " OUR "; which thinks all the time of God's world-wide purposes and of others' needs as well as our own.

(c) Liturgical prayer, in which we seek to worship with the Christian Community.

(d) Meditation, in which we think of God and seek to know more about Him and which if used rightly leads on to the prayer of affection.

(e) Contemplative meditation which ceases all thought and self-striving, and holds the truth of God's indwelling spirit in the conscious mind, while the Truth sinks into the unconscious mind and soul.

(f) The prayer of Union with God or Contemplation : when we enjoy and have fellowship with God without any thought of self.

Each of these stages in prayer enlightens the previous stages, so that when we pray for others we find ourselves holding the truth of God's purpose in our minds for them, and petition breaks into praise and thanksgiving.

None of this is achieved in a day. Only by great perseverance will we make progress. When you fail, when thoughts wander or you find yourself saying the words and thinking about something else or the mind runs back to self or you get sleepy, don't blame yourself or be troubled, just start again, even if you have to do it twenty times in ten minutes; mind control will come in time.

This is not auto-suggestion. What we allow to sink into the unconscious mind and soul is not going down into a vacuum. Because we are made in the image of God, we have capacities within us for the expression of all the qualities of God's Character and, as the Truth sinks, it calls these capacities out into expression.

" Suggestion " is not a word of accusation. It describes the way in which the mind works, and our minds work by suggestion every day. But it is always the quality of the suggestion which is important, and in deep meditation the words have the quality of Truth : and God is Truth.

## CONTEMPLATIVE MEDITATION IN GROUPS

This method of deep meditation is best learned in a group with other people, but a leader is needed who has studied and practised the method for some time. He or she will then know the dangers to be avoided and be able to help individuals in the group.

Those who start using the method are often inclined to choose sentences which they like and unless there is some discipline in this, sentences may be chosen which are centred on self, instead of on God. There should be no effort made to stir up affection or emotions of any kind. If people have feelings while they are meditating in this way they may be using psychic powers instead of surrendering all self effort. And again if someone is very neurotic or has some deeply buried complex or emotion there may be an abreaction,

13

that is an uprush of emotion, from the unconscious mind. An experienced leader would know how to help in such cases, as we shall see in the next chapter. With a leader who understands, a group can make great progress. Those who are more practised help others who are beginning : by the mere fact of the contact which there is between mind and mind in a group, they help less practised people to go deeper with them. It is important to relax before meditating, to let go of all strain, and if, during the meditation, the time seems long or you want to move, you will find that a deep breath or sigh and relaxation again enables you to go on to the end of the set time quite easily.

BE STILL AND KNOW MY INFINITE PEACE WITHIN.


## VII   ON HELPING OTHERS

Deep meditation can help us as individuals to develop our knowledge of God and leads us to deeper fellowship and union with Him in His purposes for mankind. It can also become a very valuable way of helping other people, whether they be in need of spiritual help or are ill or in need of help in any way.

We need to become aware of the way in which mind touches mind on the deep unconscious level. Many people are aware of this. We only have to think of the way in which a depressed person can spread depression, or the way in which children are quickly affected by unhappiness or quarrelling in a home, or the way in which fear can spread from one person to another, to realise that something like telepathy is real. But as Christians, we are members of the Body of Christ and there is a unity of the Spirit : in Christ we are one. It is a very close relationship.

Therefore, if we are meditating deeply and then bring a sick person " to mind " as we say, thinking for a moment of the person's name, and then continue the meditation—

14

not pushing anything into his head—but becoming deeply aware of God and of His peace or love, the person we have in mind will share what is in our mind and will be helped to an awareness of God's peace or love. God's spirit is in us both, working to overcome all evil, and our faith in God and our love can flow to the person we want to help and in that way help him to a deeper knowledge of God who is his only healer and redeemer.

This is work which a group can do, when it has learned to go really deep. There must be a deep consciousness of God in the minds of those who help in this way before such consciousness can be conveyed to anyone else. It is also the way in which blind people and people who are bedridden or old, or who have time on their hands, can help others and find in it a life of service to God. It is a method of prayer which can be used for the help of any who are in need, and a way of giving support to the Clergy and others who are on active service at home and abroad.

If we are alive to God's activity in the world, overcoming evil and working to bring His Kingdom into expression, we can have fellowship with Him in all this through meditation.

THAT THY LOVE, THY POWER, THY PEACE AND THE MIGHTINESS OF THY KINGDOM MAY BECOME KNOWN UNTO MEN.

SILENCE

If someone is neurotic or suffering from a nervous breakdown, this method of meditation can be a very real help. It will be necessary to teach it in a very simple way to begin with. The repetition of the Words of Life* will gradually change the quality of the unconscious mind and overcome and change the fear or misery buried there. In the case of a

* See my pamphlet, " How to help someone in a nervous breakdown." 6d., from the Guild of Health. (8d. by post).

long-standing neurotic case, it may be necessary to meditate regularly with the person several times a week, and then there is the possibility of an abreaction; while the person is meditating, they may suddenly have an uprush of the buried emotion from the unconscious mind. This may come out in words—" I hate my father " or " I feel so resentful I can't go on meditating." You must not disturb this effusion—let it come out even if the hatred is directed to yourself. When it has come out the person may be covered with shame, but be very gentle with him and try to help him realise that it is all coming from some past experience and is therefore not blameable, and that it is no longer necessary to feel like it. He can let it go. Help him to do this.

Then you can begin another meditation with him which aims at melting and dissolving the negative emotion which he has revealed.

" I thank Thee, Lord, that all hatred (fear, doubt, resentment, condemnation, misery or whatever else) is being melted away by the incoming of Thy love into my soul " (or it may be by the incoming of Thy Spirit of forgiveness, joy, peace and so on).

This meditation should go on for some weeks and the abreaction may occur several times before the mind is clear, but it should lead to complete recovery and happiness. If it does not, the help of a psychiatrist will be needed.

At the end of every meditation give thanks. Let the last period always be one of thanksgiving, for nothing feeds faith more than praise, adoration and thanksgiving.


## THE WORDS OF LIFE

" Be still and know that I am God " (Psalm 46[10]).
God is Love, Joy, Peace, Wisdom, Justice, Equity, Freedom, Righteousness, Life, Health, Holiness, Wholeness, Beauty, Goodness, Truth, Perfection, Knowledge, Power, which is adequacy, Faith, Calmness.

Thou art My Lord God, My King, My Saviour, My Deliverer, My Redeemer, My Healer, My Judge, My Refuge, My Stronghold, My Castle, My House of Defence, My Hope, My Glory, My Strength, My Might, and My Sure Reward.

I am the Way, The Truth, The Life, The Door, The Light, The Good Shepherd, The Bread of Life.

## ADVENT I

*Reading:* Romans 13[8-14].

*Prayer:*  Lord Jesus, our Leader, we give ourselves to Thee for the cause of Thy glorious Kingdom. Take from us all that hinders us from giving Thee our full and loyal service.

Advent calls us to the service of Christ's Kingdom. "It is high time to awake out of sleep"; Our Leader, Jesus, is at work; He came that He might destroy the works of the devil and enable us to become sons of God.

We have been called to be fellow workers with God (2 Cor. 6[1]), helping to overcome evil and to aid the fulfilment of God's good purposes for mankind. We need to know that God is at work, very deeply in our mind, so that we are alive to that truth in our daily life, able to hear His Voice and ready to respond, and aware of the evils of the world which hinder us from serving God and having fellowship with Him.

SHOW ME THY WAY, DEAR LORD, THAT I MAY WALK IN IT.

SILENCE

*Thanksgiving:*  Thou art the Way, dear Lord: I thank Thee that Thou hast called me to walk in it with Thee.

17

B

# ADVENT II

*Reading:* Romans 15[13].

*Prayer:* Blessed Lord, Who hast caused all Holy Scriptures to be written for our learning : grant that we may in such wise hear them, read, mark, learn, and inwardly digest them, that by patience and comfort of Thy Holy Word we may embrace and ever hold fast the blessed hope of Everlasting Life which Thou hast given us in Our Saviour Jesus Christ.

In the coming of God's Kingdom the whole human race will enter into and enjoy that fulness of life which Jesus calls " Everlasting Life." This has been the expectation and the hope of all faithful people from Abraham to the present day. (See Genesis 18[18-19]).

To walk " in the way of the Lord " means living in righteousness—reflecting God's own character in our way of living. The whole Bible—Old Testament and New—speaks of it. " Seek ye first the Kingdom of God and His righteousness." Only by living in this way, knowing that God is real and has a purpose for the world and for us and that He loves us and will never forsake us, can we really "be filled with joy and peace in believing " and live even in a world which has fallen away from God, in quiet confidence in Him.

I WILL NEVER LEAVE YOU NOR FORSAKE YOU;
LEARN OF ME AND LIVE.

**SILENCE**

*Thanksgiving:* Psalm 145. All Thy works praise Thee, O Lord : and Thy Saints give thanks unto Thee.

---

# ADVENT III

*Reading:* 1 Corinthians 4[1-2].

*Prayer:*  Collect for Advent III.

As Thou hast called us to Thy service, so make us worthy of the same.

St. Paul speaks of us as "the called of Jesus Christ" (Rom. 1[6]) and so we are, for by our baptism we are united to Him as members of His Body, the Church—He needs to use us as His Body to make known His purposes for mankind and the nature of His Kingdom. In the life of the Church we learn to know that His Life is ever in us with all its love and joy and peace, and to know that He works in all the world to overcome evil and to perfect His Creation. We are Ministers and Stewards of these mysteries which the world and most people around us are ignorant of : so we are not only called of Jesus Christ but sent by Him to make these mysteries known to others. We have a mission to the world and we are responsible to Christ for it. He sends us to prepare people for His Second Coming that when He comes we may be found an acceptable people in His sight. Are we awake to our calling?

WAKEN ME TO THY CALL, DEAR LORD, THAT THE KNOWLEDGE THOU HAST GIVEN ME MAY WAKEN OTHERS.

SILENCE

*Thanksgiving:*  Thank you Father for Thy Call to me— "Here am I : send me."

---

## ADVENT IV

*Reading:*  Philippians 4[4-7].

*Prayer:*  Collect for the Fourth Sunday in Advent.

In our weakness, teach us to know Thy strength.

The Advent message is almost overwhelming. God is real; He is in all the world and has a purpose for it. It is to become His Kingdom on earth like it is in Heaven, and God has called us to work with Him and eventually to share

19

in the joys of His redeemed and perfected creation. Who is worthy of such a vocation? Lord, I am not worthy. I am a sinner and I belong to a human race which has sinned and I am tainted with the sin and evil of the world. Only if Thou cleanse me and uphold me can I respond to Thy Call and give myself to the cause of Thy Kingdom.

And God does forgive : and He is our strength : and His strength will be adequate to our need, if we burn our boats and trust Him. So His peace takes possession of us and WE TRUST IN HIM AND NO LONGER IN SELF.

MY GRACE AND MERCY WILL SPEEDILY HELP AND DELIVER YOU : TRUST IN ME.

SILENCE

*Thanksgiving:* Rejoice in the Lord alway, and again I say rejoice : for God is with me.

---

# CHRISTMAS

*Reading:* Colossians 1$^{16-23}$.

*Prayer:* Though Christ, a thousand times in Bethlehem were born but not in me
'Twere all in vain,
To me reveal Thyself today, dear Lord.

The birth of Jesus was the beginning of a whole life-time of incarnation. From the moment of His birth till His resurrection, everything that He was and did and said was revealing God to us in and through our human nature. God was made flesh in Him. As we see Jesus at any moment of His life, we see something of God. As He was a helpless Babe entirely dependent upon His mother and others, so sometimes is God. We can neglect Him, crucify Him, make Him suffer as men could and did to Jesus. As He bore all suffering and prayed for His murderers and didn't want to punish, so He loves us while we are sinners and hurt and neglect Him.

But also the very fact that God was incarnate in Jesus revealed the truth that God is always like that; He is always working to reveal Himself in creation. He reveals Himself in all the beauty of unspoiled nature, in human nature at its best : yes, and in the bread and wine of the Communion.

God is light and in Him is no darkness at all, and He ever works to let His light shine out through all creation and through us in perfect goodness and love.

ARISE, SHINE : FOR THY LIGHT IS COME.

SILENCE

*Thanksgiving:* Glory be to God on high and on earth peace to men of good will. Thanks be to God.

---

## SUNDAY AFTER CHRISTMAS

*Reading:* St. John $1^{1-4}$.

*Prayer:* Jesus, born for us in Bethlehem, be to us the light of life and enlighten our understanding and our knowledge of Thee.

" In Him was life and the life was the light of men." And that life is our light now, for He dwells within us. That was the conviction of the first disciples when Jesus left them at the end. All that He had been to them during His Ministry was continuing even though they could no longer see Him in the flesh. He was that Eternal Life which was with the Father and He had been incarnate and shown to them : they had heard Him speak and had lived with Him and seen the power of that life in all His healing works and in the raising of the dead and in His own Resurrection. All this had been " the Incarnation," and now this same life is with them for evermore and is their light and will be to all generations. Christmas means all this for us. As Jesus during those years drew His disciples into the union which He had with His Father and it was lasting, so He draws us into that same union now.

BE STILL AND KNOW THAT MY LIFE, INFINITE AND
ETERNAL, IS NOW WITHIN YOU.

*Thanksgiving:* I will rejoice and give thanks unto Thee, O
Lord, for Christ, my life and my light, is born
within me.

---

## SECOND SUNDAY AFTER CHRISTMAS

*Reading:* Isaiah $60^{19\text{-}21}$.

*Prayer:* Let Thy light shine in our hearts, dear Lord, that
all darkness being dispelled, we may become
burning lights to lead others to Thee.

God willeth that He shall become known to men. Christ
came to reveal the Father. "He that hath seen Me hath
seen the Father." St. John begins his Gospel with the words
"In the beginning was the Word—in Him was life and the
life was the light of men. That was the true light which
lighteth every man." A light shines out into every corner
of a room. Light travels quickly, it penetrates; and if we
allow it, God's light will penetrate into our deep thoughts
and into the deepest part of our mind and dispel the darkness. But we must do something ourselves. We must allow
the light to sink into our minds. We do this in meditation
by finding time every day to sit and to open our minds and
allow the truth to sink deeply into the depths of our minds
that

GOD IS LIGHT WITHIN AND IN HIM IS NO DARK-
NESS AT ALL.

SILENCE

*Thanksgiving:* Thanks be to God for His love in revealing
the Truth and the Light to us.

Let Thy Light burn ever in our hearts that others may
come to know Thee through us.

---

# EPIPHANY AND FIRST SUNDAY AFTER

*Reading:* St. Matthew 2¹⁻¹².

*Prayer:* Collect for The Epiphany.

Let Thy light shine to all the nations.

Very early in our Lord's life, people from other lands came following the Star to find the Redeemer of the world and to bring their gifts into His Kingdom.

The light was not for the Jews only, and it is not for us as Christians alone.

The great and ancient religions of the world lead their adherents to seek for God and have many means of grace, but fundamentally they do not believe that God can be found or known. The " Altar to the Unknown God " in Athens and the search of the three Wise Men bear witness to this. Only through Christ can God be known, and we have received the light that we may pass it on to all the nations. This is our responsibility before God, and the reality of our prayer and the scale of our giving bear witness to the reality or not of our knowledge of the light.

THAT WE MAY PERCEIVE AND KNOW WHAT THINGS WE OUGHT TO DO, AND HAVE GRACE AND POWER TO ACHIEVE THEM.

### SILENCE

*Thanksgiving:* We give Thee thanks, dear Lord, for the light. Grant us to rejoice in its shining in other hearts.

---

## SECOND SUNDAY AFTER EPIPHANY.

*Reading:* Colossians 1⁹⁻¹⁴.

*Prayer:* Give us knowledge, dear Lord, knowledge of Thyself : that by Thy grace we may grow into Thy likeness and become Sons of God.

Our whole prayer life depends on what we believe about God—not only in our conscious mind but in the deep unconscious.

23

Wrong and unworthy ideas of God lead to ineffectiveness in prayer : so we need to search for the Truth and then to let it sink deeply into the mind. This we do in Contemplative Meditation.

Do you realise the way in which our deep minds are filled with wrong ideas and negative thoughts and feelings? It is not anything for which we can be blamed : from our earliest childhood the thoughts and ideas and the unbelief of the world around us have been soaking into us. Perhaps a lot more darkness has come in through the papers we have read and things we have heard.

The purpose of meditation is to change all this by dropping the knowledge of God into the mind, for in the soul there is the peace and love and goodness of God, if we can only know it. It is what is deep within us which comes out into expression in our life.

LET THY LIGHT SHINE WITHIN US AND DISPEL THE DARKNESS.

SILENCE

*Thanksgiving:* We give Thee thanks and glorify Thee, O Lord.

---

## THIRD SUNDAY AFTER EPIPHANY

*Reading:* St. Mark 7[18-23]. Philippians 4[8-9].

*Prayer:* Help us to think of Thee, dear Lord, for as we think, so we become.

Our whole life and way of thinking and even the healthiness of our body depends on what is stored up in our deep unconscious mind. If we have fears it is because, stored in our deep mind, there is some experience of fear. The same is true of anxiety, resentment, jealousy. And it is no good to try to fight these feelings, the only way is to change them, and it has to be done by sending down the truth that God is real and that He is Love, Forgiveness, Peace and Joy within us. His spirit can change what is dark, for He is

24

Light. The words themselves will do the work. Don't try to think—let God work.

And if you are certain that the body is always working to express what is in the deep mind, the body itself will tend to become more healed and healthy.

THAT IN MY DAILY LIFE I MAY KNOW AND TRUST THY POWER WITHIN ME.

SILENCE

*Thanksgiving:* Thanks be to God for all His love. We will have faith in Thy Life, infinite, eternal, overmastering, at work within us.

---

## FOURTH SUNDAY AFTER EPIPHANY

*Reading:* St. John 17$^{20-23}$.

*Prayer:* Speak, Lord, to my soul.

We are learning to wait on God—to listen, not with our outward ears, but with our soul. God does not speak aloud to us, nor do we know at once what He says to us. It becomes clear to us gradually or sometimes in a flash of conviction or illumination. But, for this to happen, we need to be certain of God—to know that He is real—to know Him intuitively. We learn this by waiting in silence to let Him make Himself known to us.

We come to this gradually as we persevere, first, thinking about God, as Jesus often did, in the grass, in the lilies, in nature and then in us, so realising our unity with Him : " I pray that they may be one in us. I in them and Thou in them." Jesus was never self-conscious, He was always God-conscious—so we wait on God that we may become like Him.

THY SPIRIT IS WITHIN ME, DEAR LORD. I ADORE THEE.

SILENCE

*Thanksgiving:* Blessed and praised be the Father of our
Lord Jesus Christ who ever willeth to make Himself known to us. Thanks be to God.

## FIFTH SUNDAY AFTER EPIPHANY

*Reading:* : St. John 14[15-20].
*Prayer:* Holy Spirit of God, ever dwelling within us and
around us, come forth now into expression in our
lives.

God's Holy Spirit is always within us and around us.
" Ye know Him for He dwelleth with you and shall be in
you."

And the Holy Spirit is all that God is. He is creative
—always at work in all the world—in all creation bringing
order out of chaos. He is *Redemptive*—always working
to overcome all evil. He is the Sanctifyer—always working to perfect all things—working to make us like God.
So, in meditation, we keep still and become aware of His
presence within us and wait for Him to work. This is not
easy at first, but gradually we learn not to try to do something ourselves, not to think, not to imagine, not to stir any
feelings but to let the Holy Spirit work in us. If we learn
to do this, the Holy Spirit will bring forth fruit in us and
we will grow in the love and peace of God.

MY SPIRIT IS LOVE AND JOY AND PEACE WITHIN.

SILENCE

*Thanksgiving:* Eternal Goodness, Thou wilt never leave me
nor forsake me. Thanks be to God.

## SIXTH SUNDAY AFTER EPIPHANY

*Reading:* The Epistle for the Day. 1 St. John 3[1].
*Prayer:* The Collect for the Day.

For this purpose the Son of God was manifested : that
He might destroy the works of the devil. It is Christ's work
to destroy all evil in order that God's perfect goodness may

prevail in us and in all the world; and that we might become Sons of God, growing into His likeness and sharing with Him the life of His eternal and glorious Kingdom. It is to this that we are called as Christians. St. Paul speaks of us as " the Called of Jesus Christ." Can we become worthy of such a high calling? Only if we allow the Holy Spirit to enter deeply into our hearts and minds to change what is dark and evil there. We can become what God has made us to become if we want to, but it means giving time each day to wait on God and to let the truth of His indwelling sink deeply enough into the mind to cleanse it and to teach us to know Him.

NOW ARE WE SONS OF GOD. HIS LIFE IS IN US.

SILENCE

*Thanksgiving:* As for me, I will uphold Thy presence in righteousness and when I wake up after Thy likeness I will be satisfied with it. Thanks be to God.

---

## SEPTUAGESIMA SUNDAY

*Reading:* St. John 15⁴⁻⁸.

*Prayer:* Infinite Spirit, my Creator, I adore Thee with deep humility.

God is greater than all the creation which He has made and He is perfect in His Whole Being. Yet it is true that He is within me.

The secret of life is to become aware of Him and to learn to abide in Him.

How can we do this? On the surface of our minds we move from one thought to another: we can't be always thinking of God. Yet underneath there is an undercurrent of feeling which is always there.

If you are in love, you do your work and you think about it, you are not thinking of your loved one all the time; if you did, you would make mistakes in your work; and yet, deep down in your mind, your love is there—you abide in it all the time. So sometimes, we abide in misery or anxiety or bitterness.

But so also we can learn to abide in God. If He becomes real to your deep mind you will abide in Him. And, of course, He abides in you.

I AM WITH YOU ALWAYS AND THAT MEANS NOW.

SILENCE

*Thanksgiving:* My Lord and my God, I praise and worship and glorify Thee for ever.

---

## SEXAGESIMA SUNDAY

*Reading:* St. John 15[4-5].

*Prayer:*    Abide in me, dear Lord, and teach me to abide in Thee.

If we learn really to abide in Christ, to be deeply aware of Him, we have found the secret of Christian living. It can only come by persevering in meditation in which we learn to wait on Him, and to let Him make Himself known to us. Then the deep mind becomes full of the knowledge of Christ within. As we learn to wait on Him in this way, we become healed of all that is dark in thought and feeling, and into its place comes light and love and joy.

Just as when we are in love with someone we are content to rest lovingly in his presence and heart talks to heart, so it can be with Christ. And as we do so, our mind becomes attuned to His mind—" Let this mind be in you which was also in Christ." Then His thoughts become our thoughts and gradually His character grows in us. And the more this happens, the more we share in His purposes and plans for the world.

ABIDE LOVINGLY IN ME AND KNOW MY PEACE.

SILENCE

*Thanksgiving:* O Lord, our Redeemer, how excellent is Thy name in all the world.

# QUINQUAGESIMA SUNDAY

*Reading:* 1 Corinthians 12$^{31}$ and 13$^{1-13}$.

*Prayer:* Unto Thee, O Lord, will I lift up my soul. Lead me forth in Thy truth, and learn me.

Wednesday is Ash Wednesday, the first day of Lent: a time of discipline, during which we try to prepare for Good Friday and Easter.

Many Christians think of Lent as a time of struggle—to be good—to give up something which we like—to do more —to strive more in prayer.

Try, for a change, to do the opposite. God is with us and in us always. He is holy, good, loving. He is peace, and joy, and wisdom, and life and goodness. All these are in Him and therefore in us—now. " Son, thou art ever with Me, and all that I have is thine." (St. Luke 15$^{31}$).

Try to let go of all effort, of all striving : let go of self and wait on God, and let Him make Himself and what He is known to us.

To do this, we must make time—by talking less—by reading the paper much less—by being quicker over meals. Then get quiet—in church—in a bus—in a train—in your room. Sit and relax and then let go of self—let go any hatred, jealousy, resentment, fear. Then accept God's forgiveness and then be still and repeat over and over again :

GIVE ME KNOWLEDGE OF THY LOVE WITHIN, DEAR LORD.

### SILENCE

*Thanksgiving:* I will give thanks unto Thee, O Lord, for Thou hast heard my prayer.

# LENT I

*Reading:* Isaiah 6¹⁻⁹.

*Prayer:* Grant me, dear Lord, a deeper knowledge of Thy Holy Spirit within and around me, that I may hear more clearly Thy Voice within, calling me to Thy service.

In his vision, Isaiah realised that God was not only high and lifted up, greater than all Creation, but that His Spirit filled the whole earth. In this realised glory of God he saw himself, and knew that he was a sinner needing to be cleansed. He also realised the sinfulness of his own nation and God's concern about it. So he hears God's call, " Who will go for us?" And he answers, " Here am I, send me."

God is the same today. He is concerned about the world. Now be still and say over quietly and slowly :

WHO WILL GO FOR US? O LORD GOD, HERE AM I.

### SILENCE

*Thanksgiving:* Thanks be to God on High, and in me.

---

# LENT II

*Reading:* St. John 17¹⁻³.

*Prayer:* Wait thou still upon the Lord and He will give thee thy heart's desire. So help us to wait on Thee, dear Lord.

Jesus said : This is Life Eternal, that they may know Thee, the only true God, and Him whom thou didst send, even Jesus (St. John 17³). And this is the aim of meditation. All wrong religion comes from wrong ideas of God.

Our knowledge of God must come from Him. We have our own ideas about God. We think that we know what His peace, His love, His wisdom are like, but it is no good meditating just on our own ideas. We must learn to wait on God and to be taught of Him by His Holy Spirit within. So, wait in humility. Don't think about the words, say them over and over slowly, receptively. If any thoughts come—let them go. Wait on God.

GIVE ME KNOWLEDGE, DEAR LORD. KNOWLEDGE
OF THYSELF.

SILENCE

*Thanksgiving:* We thank Thee, dear Lord, for Thy Presence with us always.

---

## LENT III

*Reading:* 1 John 1$^{1-4}$.

*Prayer:* Speak, Lord, to my soul, and teach me to listen.

The Christian religion is a way of life: a life lived in consciousness of Christ within—not like a bird in a cage—but a life coming into expression; incarnating itself in us day by day in our ordinary life.

Jesus was always to the early Christians " the Christ," the leader to the Kingdom of God. " They preached Jesus, that He is the Christ." (Acts 5$^{42}$, 8$^5$, 9$^{22}$, 17$^3$, 18$^{28}$). He had brought the life of the Kingdom into expression in the world. They had seen its power in all His healing, His raising of the dead. His own resurrection was the assurance that this life was now within them and available to them, with all its power. " I live, yet not I, but Christ liveth in me." (Gal. 2$^{20}$).

To know the power of that Life is possible for us now.

THAT I MAY KNOW HIM, AND THE POWER OF HIS
RISEN LIFE WITHIN ME.

SILENCE

*Thanksgiving:* Jesu My Lord, I Thee adore. I give Thee thanks.

---

## LENT IV

*Reading:* St. John 14$^{16-20}$.

31

*Prayer:*   Holy Spirit of God, ever dwelling within us, lead
us into deeper truth.

St. Paul says: "You ought to know by this time that
Christ is in you, unless you are not real Christians at all."*
But do we? Not unless we train ourselves day by day in
meditation to know Him. It won't come by our own efforts,
but if we learn to be still and wait on Him, He will teach
us. So we must be still, saying the words over receptively.
Then the knowledge of His presence grows in our hearts
and minds. It is not an emotional, not a visual knowledge
but a spiritual one. So don't try to force it. In fact, don't
try to do anything but wait on God. Don't expect to have
any feelings or visions—they are no sure sign of saintliness
and are often a temptation to pride. When our Lord becomes more real, rejoice in Him and give thanks.

QUICKEN THOU MY FAITH IN THEE, THAT I MAY
KNOW THY PRESENCE.

SILENCE

*Thanksgiving:* Thanks be to God for His great love to me.

---

## LENT V

*Reading:* Ephesians 3$^{14-19}$.
*Prayer:*   Give me knowledge, dear Lord, knowledge of
Thyself.

In Jesus dwelleth "all the fulness of God." In Him we
see the love of God revealed. But more than that: in Him
we see that it always has been God's nature to express Himself. In the Blessed Trinity the Father expressed Himself in
the Son—His eternal Word, and the Word responded to the
Father's love and expressed Him. Abraham realised that
he could only please God by expressing God's character in
righteousness. Jesus expressed God. "He that hath seen
me hath seen the Father." So, in the Church, God ex-

* 2 Corinthians 13$^5$. J. B. Phillips' *The New Testament in Modern
English* (Geoffrey Bles, 4d.).

presses Himself in the Sacraments, and you and I are made by Him to express His life and character and to grow into His likeness. So in silence we wait on Him to do what He ever does to express Himself in us. He can do it by His spirit within us. We can't do it ourselves.

THOU ART EVER WITH ME. ALL THAT I HAVE IS THINE.

SILENCE

*Thanksgiving:* My Lord, My God, I adore Thee. I give Thee thanks.

---

## PALM SUNDAY.  LENT VI

*Reading:* St. Luke 23$^{33-35}$ and Psalm 22$^{11-19}$.

*Prayer:*     I will magnify Thee, O God, my King, and I will praise Thy name for ever and ever. Every day will I give thanks unto Thee and praise Thy name for ever and ever.

This week we are to see Eternal Love dealing with sin and evil. St. John says that Christ was manifested " that He might destroy the works of the Devil " (1 John 3$^8$); and on the Cross He did it, in order to show us how God overcomes evil. And what do we see? Eternal love suffering the worst that men can do to Him, without any desire to punish them. He suffers the evil Himself and refuses to let it find any response in Himself and so He redeems it and ends it. " Father, forgive them, for they know not what they do."

That is God's way of overcoming evil and it is shown to us on the Cross. God loved us that much. In fact it was when we were sinners that He sought us out and was prepared to die for us. It cost Him that to redeem us from the power of evil.

And what we see in the Cross is still God's way with evil. It makes Him suffer now whenever we sin or become involved in the sin of the world. Can we forgive as He does and be like Him?

33

c

FATHER, I FORGIVE, I FORGIVE, I WANT TO FOR-
GIVE AS YOU FORGIVE.

SILENCE

*Thanksgiving:* Lord Jesus, our Leader, we give ourselves to
Thee for joy or for sorrow, for success or for
failure, for life or for death, now and for evermore.

---

## GOOD FRIDAY: THE CROSS

*Reading:* Mark 14$^{32-42}$.

*Prayer:* Strengthen, we beseech Thee, O Lord, the wills
of Thy faithful people that we, ardently with-
standing the evils of this world, may rejoice in the
fellowship of Thy Kingdom.

We live in a world which is out of harmony with God:
it is a fallen creation, it has " missed the mark and fallen
short " of God's purpose of expressing His own perfection
and glory. Evil has become very strong and from our birth
we have been surrounded and affected by it and involved in
it. In our deep unconscious minds are buried the negative
ideas, the unbelief, and the wrong values of the fallen
creation: we need to be reconciled to God, i.e. healed and
redeemed and saved from our condition. Only God can do
this. In Gethsemane Jesus faced all this evil; His whole life
and character had condemned it and now the resentment
aroused is about to kill Him and He knows it and His
human nature shrinks from it. He faces crucifixion in the
knowledge of His Father's love and purpose and will to
overcome all evil and to do it by suffering and so to bring
good out of evil. Nevertheless " not My will but Thine be
done." It was a cry of victory and obedience. For the joy
that was set before Him, He endured the Cross. It was the
joy of doing the Father's will, triumphing over evil by
suffering, not by punishment, and of thus bringing God's

Kingdom into being. For this joy He endured the Cross. With Him, and in Him, you and I can do the same. He calls us to challenge evil and to overcome evil with Him and for His Kingdom.

THAT I MAY KNOW HIM AND THE POWER OF HIS RESURRECTION AND THE FELLOWSHIP OF HIS SUFFERING.

SILENCE

*Thanksgiving:* We thank Thee, blessed Lord, for Thy courage, Thy victory and Thy obedience.

---

## EASTER

*Reading:* St. Luke 24[41]. St. John 16[20-22]. Romans 14[17].
*Prayer:* Let Thy love, Thy power and the mightiness of Thy Kingdom be known to all people.

Easter is a time of rejoicing. Not only because, by the perfect obedience to His Father's will, Jesus had triumphed over all evil and broken the power of sin and opened the way to the life of the Kingdom : but He has done all this for us so that we may share in it all. To be a Christian means being made one with Christ, a member of His Body, having His life within us and therefore sharing all that He is and all that He has done. As St. Paul says, He hath made us fit to be partakers of the inheritance of the Saints in Light, he hath delivered us out of the power of darkness, he hath brought us into the Kingdom of His dear Son, in whom we have redemption, the forgiveness of our sins (Ccl. 1[12-14]).

All this has been done for us on the Cross and is now ours by the Resurrection; Jesus is now the risen, crucified Christ, the leader to the Kingdom, who will always be with us and in us. Rejoice! And just because this union with the crucified, risen Christ is so real, we too are risen to new possibilities of life and power and faith. " Because I live,

35

ye shall live also," said Jesus; and St. Paul says, " In Christ shall all be made alive." " He that believeth in ME hath passed from death into life." Think on these things—meditate : let the truth of them sink deeply. They are words of life by which we can become alive.

THAT I MAY KNOW HIM AND THE POWER OF HIS RISEN LIFE RISING UP WITHIN ME.

*Thanksgiving:* Thou art the King of Glory, O Christ. Thou art the everlasting Son of the Father. When Thou hadst overcome the sharpness of death, Thou didst open the Kingdom of Heaven to all believers.

---

## EASTER I

*Reading:* Ephesians $5^{23-32}$.

*Prayer:* Grant, O Lord, that as the Body of Christ we may grow unto a full grown man, unto the measure of the stature of the fulness of Christ.

Our Lord's unity with us is very real. He says, " I am the vine and ye are the branches : he that abideth in ME and I in him beareth much fruit, for apart from Me ye can do nothing." The life of the tree is in every branch and leaf, expressing itself in life and beauty and fruit.

So also the Church is the Body of Christ and the life of the head is in every member of the body. At our baptism we were made members of Christ's Body. " Know ye not that your bodies are members of Christ?" (1 Cor. $6^{15}$) and " We are His flesh and His bones " (Eph. $5^{30}$). The Church is not the building but the people, whose bodies are members of the Body which " is Christ " in action worshipping the Father through and with them and wanting to use them as a body to redeem the world and to heal. We will never know this till we let the truth of it sink into our deep minds.

To believe in Christ means believing this and it means our passing from deadness to life.

THAT AS MEMBERS OF CHRIST'S BODY WE MAY PASS FROM DEATH INTO LIFE NOW.

SILENCE

*Thanksgiving:* I thank Thee, dear Lord, that I can know Him and the power of His resurrection within.

---

## EASTER II

*Reading:* Colossians $1^{3-4, 9-18}$

*Prayer:* O God, who in a holy meal has given unto us a foretaste of Thy Kingdom, open our eyes to the full meaning of this sacred mystery.

The Church gathered together for worship " is Christ " (1 Cor. $12^{12}$). He takes the bread and breaks it that He may fill His Body with His Life, that it may be one body filled with His strength. If any member of this body is sick, or stays away through carelessness or lack of love, it is Christ who suffers in His Body. Yet we, as members of His Body, also suffer, for they are members of our Body. " If one member suffers, all the members suffer with it. If one member is honoured all rejoice " (1 Cor. $12^{26}$). So we should care for one another, and ' care ' means love. Christ loves His Body and cares for every member and fills the whole Body with His Life that it may be without blemish, a Body fit for His use. So in Communion we are given " The Body of our Lord Jesus Christ " . . . " to preserve thy body and soul unto Everlasting Life "—that is, to fulness of life, and we are told to feed on Him in our hearts by faith and be thankful. Christ in us and we in Him.

I WILL FEED ON HIM IN MY HEART AND BE THANKFUL.

SILENCE

*Thanksgiving:* And here we offer and present unto Thee, O Lord, ourselves, our souls, and bodies to be Thy lively Body. Thanks be to God.

---

## EASTER III

*Reading:* St. John 5[19-29].
*Prayer:*　O, lead me forth in Thy Truth and learn me. (Psalm 25[4]).

When Jesus spoke of death, He used the word in two ways. Sometimes He meant those who had passed into the next life through physical death, but more often He meant those who were ignorant of God and who were living as if God did not exist. Life as most people in the world live it is not life but death. God may be all round us and in us, yet we can be blind to Him. " He was in the world and the world knew Him not " (St. John 1[10]). But to know God and to believe in Him is to enter into life : to have our eyes open to truth. Meditation aims at a deeper knowledge of God : not only knowing about Him but knowing Him in our own experience as His life quickens all that is of God in us and we really enter into His peace and joy and love. But this can only happen if we allow the truth of His life within us to sink very deeply into our minds till all that is not of God within us has been changed, and the aggregate of the thought in our deep minds is of Him and of His Spirit within.

QUICKEN THE POWER OF THY LIFE WITHIN ME, THAT I MAY LIVE TO THY GLORY.

### SILENCE

*Thanksgiving:* I will give thanks unto Thee, O Lord, with my whole heart, I will sing praise unto Thee. When I called upon Thee, Thou heardest me and enduest my soul with much strength. (Psalm 138).

## EASTER IV

*Reading:* Isaiah 48[6-11].

*Prayer:* Show me Thy Way, O Lord, and teach me Thy
Paths.

Even on the natural level of life we may be blind to what
is real. Some are colour blind, some have no ear for music
and can't distinguish tunes. Others have no appreciation
of poetry. To them these aspects of life are unreal. Yet in
some such cases if the persons attention is drawn to it, they
can become aware of it. So to many people God seems unreal. They have heard a great deal about Him, but He is
not real in their experience. Meditation can develop a new
faculty within us by which we become aware of God and
we know Him. Our eyes are open to Him within us, and if
we persevere His presence with us becomes intuitive. Every
time we meditate we store up knowledge of His love and
joy and peace and wisdom, and as this knowledge accumu-
lates in the deep mind it begins to come out into expression
in our character, so that we become calmer and have a sense
of peace. We become more loving in our personal relationships, and so on. In time it affects the body as well, giving
us an experience of a higher quality of physical life, fulness
of life and greater resistance to illness. We are then expressing His risen Life, that Life which in Him healed the sick
to the glory of God.

I WOULD BE ALIVE WITH THY LIFE, DEAR LORD.

SILENCE

*Thanksgiving:* And now, Lord, what is my hope? Truly
my hope is in Thee. Thanks be to God.

---

## EASTER V. ROGATION

*Reading:* St. John 11[42].

*Prayer:* Unto Thee, O Lord, will I lift up my soul.
My God, I will put my trust in Thee for ever.

The word " rogation " means asking, and it is natural for children to ask their Father for things which they need; but asking is not enough by itself. If God is to answer, we must listen. That means putting a stop to all our asking and thinking, and waiting while the person we have spoken to replies by putting his thoughts into our minds. Do we ever do this? Can you still your mind and wait on God while He makes His will and purpose known to you? So many people go on talking to God all the time and never wait on Him or give Him a chance to reply. Jesus knew that God always hears. How can He help doing so when He is always in us? " Your Father knoweth what you need before you ask Him " (St. Matthew 6[8]). The question is not, " Does God hear us? " but " Do we listen to Him?" And we listen not with our ears, nor with our mind, but in silent waiting on God with our soul. Can we learn to wait on Him in this way? It will need a lot of perseverance to do it, but it is greatly worth while.

WAIT THOU STILL UPON GOD AND HE WILL
RENEW THY STRENGTH.

**SILENCE**

*Thanksgiving:* We thank Thee, O Lord, that they who wait on Thee shall renew their strength.

---

## OUR LORD'S ASCENSION

*Reading:* Ephesians 4[4-13].

*Prayer:* Ascended Lord, grant us in heart and mind with Thee to dwell.

Our Lords Ascension was not a departure. He ascended " that He might fill all things " (Eph. 4[9-10]). The incarnation was not a visit from a far distant heaven. It was the revelation of God within His creation : His life fills both heaven and earth. So our Lord's ascension is the assurance of His promise, " Lo, I am with you always," and " Ye know Him, for He dwelleth with you and shall be in you." He ascended that He might be one with God who is "the Father above all, through all and in you all " (Eph. 4⁶).

Do we know this indwelling? Yes, intellectually. But not deeply enough to affect our whole life, unless we learn to silence the conscious mind and let the truth of Christ's indwelling fill our deepest mind and soul and let God Himself speak to us and make Himself known to us. Then we will know Him intuitively. There will be no need for us to be thinking constantly about Him. His power will be in us and will work through us.

## QUICKEN THOU MY FAITH IN THY PRESENCE WITHIN ME.

### SILENCE

*Thanksgiving:* Jesus, ascended Lord, I adore Thee.

---

## SUNDAY AFTER THE ASCENSION

*Reading:* St. John 14¹⁵⁻²⁶.
*Prayer:* Holy Spirit, speak to my soul.

Jesus took much trouble to teach His disciples about the indwelling of the Holy Spirit. They had learned to love Him and to rely on His presence. Now He is leaving them but the Holy Spirit is to be His presence within them. After the coming of the Holy Spirit they knew that to be true. He is with them for ever. His promise had been, " I will not leave you comfortless, I will come to you," and it was true.

He had said, " The Son doeth nothing but what He seeth the Father doing." " I and my Father are one." Now He makes it clear that Father, Son and Holy Spirit are one ever present power with and within them. Jesus had said, " All power hath been given unto Me in heaven and on earth," and now that power is in them and " the works that I do shall ye do, and greater works shall ye do because I go to the Father." This is the fulfilment of the promise that " the Father and I will come and make our abode in him " (St. John 14$^{23}$) and " that they may be one in us : I in them and Thou in them, that they may be one in us " (St. John 17$^{21-23}$). This is what St. Peter meant when He spoke of Jesus ascending that " He might fill all things." Our Lord's Ascension was not a departure. It was a continuing presence which is still the truth for us today.

I AM THE ASCENDED CHRIST WITHIN YOU.

*Thanksgiving:* Praise the Lord, O my soul, and all that is within me, praise His Holy Name.

---

## WHITSUN

*Reading:* St. John 14$^{16-24}$ and 17$^{21-23}$.

*Prayer:*    Holy Spirit of God ever dwelling within us and around us, we adore Thee with deep humility.

The Holy Spirit is the Spirit of Christ. " I will not leave you comfortless; I will come to you " (St. John 14$^{17}$). At Whitsun this promise was fulfilled.

We are told that God's spirit fills both heaven and earth. His spirit is in all life, in the grass and flowers, in every cell of life in our bodies. That is the creative spirit which ever works to express itself in perfection and wholeness. But God is not only in us, He is greater than all and perfect in Himself apart from Creation, and therefore He also pours His holy spirit upon us, as He did upon the prophets and upon the Virgin Mary. In fact, whenever He calls anyone to do any work for Him, He pours His Holy spirit on them to enable them to do what He calls them to do. So when the Holy Spirit came at Whitsun, it came to enable the Church to be the Spirit-filled Body of Christ. He comes at Confirmation to enable us to act as full members of His Body. He comes at ordination to enable Deacons, Priests and

Bishops to fulfil their functions in the Church wisely. So we need to learn to be aware of His Spirit given to us and already within us, and we do so in meditation. St. Paul calls us "the called of Jesus Christ" (Rom. 1⁶) and God gives the Holy Spirit to them that are called.

THAT I MAY KNOW HIM WHO CALLS ME AND HIS POWER WORKING WITHIN ME.

SILENCE

*Thanksgiving:* Glory be to the Father and to the Son and to the Holy Ghost. Blessed for evermore.

---

## TRINITY SUNDAY

*Reading:* Isaiah 6¹⁻⁸.

*Prayer:* Most Holy Trinity, one God in three persons, Spirit of love, of justice, of comradeship and of freedom, we believe that Thou art here present in us and around us. We adore Thee with deep humility. We desire above all to be united with Thee in Thy purposes of love and goodness for all mankind.

The doctrine of the Trinity is an attempt to put into words what we believe to be the nature of God. God is love (1 St. John 4⁸). And love cannot exist in isolation. Love must love, and that love must be responded to and expressed. So the Father loved, and the Son responded to His love and expressed it. Then the spirit of love went from the Father to the Son and from the Son to the Father, binding them in a unity, unbroken and indivisible.

" My Father and I are one " (St. John 10³⁰).

" The Son doeth nothing but what He seeth the Father doing " (St. John 5¹⁹).

And as the Son was ever expressing the Father by giving back to Him a worthy expression of Himself, so the Son carried this expressing of the Father out into time and space in creation, which was made by Him (St. John 1³).

All creation is made to worship God.

" All the earth doth worship Thee." (The *Te deum*).

The time is coming when all men will worship the Father in Spirit and in Truth (St. John 4²³).

WE WORSHIP AND ADORE THEE, O GOD.

SILENCE

*Thanksgiving:* Great is the Lord and marvellous, worthy to be praised. There is no end of His greatness.

---

## TRINITY I

*Reading:* Romans 12¹⁻².

*Prayer:* That I may be holy and whole as Thou art whole.

God is not only morally and spiritually holy, He is complete in His entire Being, and therefore whole as well as holy. And you cannot imagine a holy and whole Father of mankind who would not wish His children to grow like Him not only in holiness but in wholeness. It is therefore God's purpose that we shall be whole in soul and mind and body. And as the mind and the soul are always expressing their condition in the body, we need to be healed of all the diseases of the soul and mind. This can only come about as the complete and perfect life of God cleanses and heals us in the deep unconscious mind and soul as we let His spirit fill us and transform us.

BE YE TRANSFORMED BY THE RENEWING OF
YOUR MIND AND BE WHOLE.

SILENCE

*Thanksgiving:* Holy, Holy, Holy is the Lord of Hosts,
The whole earth is full of Thy glory.

---

## TRINITY II

*Reading:* St. John 1⁹⁻¹⁴.

*Prayer:* Father, we would worship Thee.

God is always working to express Himself. Wherever any part of creation expresses, even in a small way, something of the beauty or perfection or peace or wisdom of God, it worships Him. It gives back to Him a worthy expression of some aspect of His Being : it responds to Him and that is worship. So the hills, the sky, the beauty of nature and, finally, man are made to worship God. It is the purpose of meditation so to receive into our minds and souls the truth of God's love and peace and joy that the quality of His character may grow in us and express itself through us, that we may worship God—not in word alone—in our lives and characters. "As many as received Him, to them He gave the right to become the children of God."

In meditation we open ourselves to receive Him.

ALL THE EARTH DOTH WORSHIP THEE,
THE FATHER EVERLASTING.

SILENCE

*Thanksgiving:* We praise Thee, O God, we acknowledge Thee to be the Lord. We give Thee thanks.

---

## TRINITY III

*Reading:* St. Matthew 15[18-20].
*Prayer:* I would learn of Thee, Holy Spirit within, and know Thy peace.

We all need cleansing on the deep levels of the unconscious mind and soul. There is much darkness there. It is not necessarily due to our own sin. A great deal of it is "worldliness" : negative feeling, unbelief, failure to expect the best, fear due to lack of faith, thinking the worst of others, ignorance of God, which is worldliness. All this has been soaking into most of our deep minds ever since our birth and we are unaware of it. Yet this is the biggest hindrance to a simple faith in God, and to our peace. In meditation we allow the truth about God to soak into our minds day by day. As the light of God's reality, love, joy, peace fills the deep mind it changes the darkness and fills the soul with light.

It is a slow process but we must go on, expecting no feelings, no uplift. Everything is working on a level below consciousness, but it *is* working.

LET THY LIGHT SHINE THROUGH MY DARKNESS,
DEAR LORD.

SILENCE

*Thanksgiving:* In Thy light shall we see light.
We praise Thee, O Lord.

---

## TRINITY IV

*Reading:* Lamentations 3$^{25\text{-}26}$.
*Prayer:* Speak to my heart, Lord Jesus, and teach me to know Thee.

In this kind of meditation we are learning to wait on God, and to be taught by Him. We don't expect Him to speak in words which we can hear with our ears : He speaks to the heart. We don't expect to have feelings. But when later, as we persevere, we find we are less fussy and calmer in all we do, and when we are less upset by other people and have a deeper love in personal relationship, then we know that He has spoken and taught us. Some people may have experiences of great peace or joy, but if so, thank God for it and don't talk about it, let it grow within you. Try to let go of self and be very humble.

If you don't have any feelings, thank God still more, and know that God is working in you, and the day will come when you will have evidence that the fruit of the spirit is growing within. Don't try to concentrate, try to let go and wait on God and let Him work within you.

JESUS, SAVIOUR, THOU KNOWEST THAT I LOVE
THEE—SPEAK TO MY HEART.

*Thanksgiving:* My Lord and My God, I praise and thank
Thee.

---

## TRINITY V

*Reading:* Acts $5^{42}$, $8^5$, $9^{22}$, $17^3$, $18^{28}$.

*Prayer:* Lord Jesus, our Leader, we give ourselves to Thee
for the cause of Thy glorious Kingdom.

Always in our meditation we need to remember that Jesus
is " the Christ," the Leader to the Kingdom of God on
earth, the Redeemer, who is overcoming all evil through us,
who won the victory over evil on the Cross and is alive now.
The first disciples preached Jesus that He is the Christ.

This will save us from a great mistake, from being piet-
istic or indulging in quietism. We are not escaping from
the world " into God." We are called to work with God in
His purposes for the world. It is not enough to think of
" Jesus only." " God so loved the world " that He sent
Jesus to redeem it.

The Eastern religions are all escapist. The Christian
religion is the only religion which gives hope of overcoming
all evil and of fulfilling God's purpose for the world. So
when we say " Lord Christ within, I adore Thee," we
should be aware of Christ's life working in all the world
and in all the people of the world and yet within. To know
this, is the very heart of the Christian religion.

LORD CHRIST WITHIN, QUICKEN THOU MY FAITH
IN THEE.

SILENCE

*Thanksgiving:* Lord Christ within, I adore Thee.
I praise and thank Thee.

# TRINITY VI

*Reading:* 1 John 1$^{1-4}$.

*Prayer:* Lord, Thou hast been our refuge from one genera-
tion to another. Before the mountains were brought
forth or ever the earth and the world were made :
Thou art from everlasting and world without end.
Therefore will I trust Thee.

To know that Jesus is " the Word of God," and that " all
things were made by Him," and that He is also within the
world and in us now, ought to fill us with joy and confidence. There is meaning in life and purpose. God is real
and at work. It is worth while praying and living. And
because this Christ is the Jesus of the Gospels, we know that
He is also deeply simple and human and friendly. " I have
called you friends." He is one whom we can trust.

So, again and again we turn to the inner sanctuary of
our souls and find Him and rejoice in His love and peace.
Do let your heart sing for joy of Christ, even in the midst
of trials. And even if you have not got to that stage, begin
to act as if you had got to it. Rejoice in Him and give Him
thanks.

Then you will face life, and the world as it is, anew.
Yes, there are the facts, all the difficulties and the miseries
and so on : but there is now also the Truth—Jesus is with
us and is adequate to our need.

BE STILL AND REJOICE IN MY PRESENCE,
I AM WITH YOU ALWAYS.

**SILENCE**

*Thanksgiving:* Thanks be to God for His great gift.

---

# TRINITY VII

*Reading:* Ephesians 3$^{14}$ to end.

*Prayer:* Deepen our faith in Thy presence within us, dear
Lord, that Thy light may shine through us for the
help of others.

Jesus is "the Christ," working in all the world to fulfil God's purposes of perfection, to bring His Kingdom on earth. And it is this Jesus who is in us, almost like a prisoner sometimes, waiting to be released into expression in us. As the life of a bulb in winter waits for the conditions which will enable it to express itself in all the beauty of the flower, so Jesus is in us now.

It is in meditation that we open ourselves to let His life and character come forth in us. His love and light and peace become manifest in our lives. And when this happens we become more aware of the sin and misery and unbelief, the negative attitudes, the disease of the world we live in, and realise how Christ is imprisoned and crucified afresh, and how deeply He needs our witness to the truth.

Someone's marriage is in a tangle. "It's a hopeless situation"; but is it? If God is real and Christ within? The doctor says of someone, "this is inoperable and incurable; he's going to die"—but is he? If Christ within works, as He did on earth, healing, raising the dead, stilling the storm : is God less powerful today? Can we become God-centred instead of self-centred? And know the truth, and trust in Him?

SAVE ME FROM SELF, DEAR LORD : I WOULD
TRUST IN THEE ALONE.

**SILENCE**

*Thanksgiving:* Father, I thank Thee that Thou hast heard me, and I know that Thou dost always hear me.

---

## TRINITY VIII

*Reading:* St. John 14$^{25\text{-}31}$.

*Prayer:* O Lord Jesus, who saidst unto Thy disciples, "Peace I leave with you : My peace I give unto you," regard not our sins but the faith of Thy Church, and grant us to know Thy peace.

49

We all have our own idea of peace. It is generally the idea of escape, from war, from tiredness, from noise. God's idea of peace is different. We can only know it if God Himself teaches us. " Peace I leave with you : My peace I give unto you." Jesus said this just before He went out on the way to Gethsemane. There was no escape for Him. How can we learn it? Only by surrendering all our own striving, and in deep humility waiting on Him to teach us in the depths of our souls. But however much we may have previously learned, what He teaches will be new. As with our Lord, it will be a deep peace which enables us to rest in Him, quite certain that He is adequate to our need whatever it may be. The last words spoken before the Cross and the first word to His disciples after His resurrection were of peace. And in the world as it is, with all its fears of the future, with one person out of twenty having to go to Mental Hospitals, and one marriage out of twelve becoming broken, how much we need His peace. If only the Church, every member of it, could radiate peace in the world, what a power it could become! But this will only be, if the peace of God has filled our hearts as we wait on Him and let the concept of peace sink into our souls.

GRANT THAT IN MY DAILY LIFE I MAY KNOW THY PEACE WITHIN.

SILENCE

*Thanksgiving:* I thank Thee, dear Lord, that Thou art teaching me to know Thy peace within.

## TRINITY IX

*Reading:* St. John 14$^{16-20}$.

*Prayer:* Holy Spirit, speak to my soul.

Jesus took a lot of trouble to teach His disciples to believe in the indwelling of His Holy Spirit and to know that the Holy Spirit was His Spirit. " I will not leave you comfortless : I will come to you." The Doctrine of the Blessed

Trinity does not teach us to think of three separate Beings. Jesus said, " I and My Father are one." He never did anything without the Father doing it with Him. "The Son doeth nothing but what He seeth the Father doing " (St. John 5$^{19}$).

Try to realise this unity in God, because then we know all the power of God is with us and within us always and we can learn to trust it. But this truth must sink deeply into the mind so that we really know it in every circumstance of life.

I AM THE HOLY SPIRIT, GOD WITHIN YOU.

SILENCE

*Thanksgiving:* Glory be to the Father and to the Son and to the Holy Ghost now present, within and around me. Thanks be to God.

---

## TRINITY X

*Reading:* St. John 16$^{13-15}$.

*Prayer:* " Call upon ME in the time of trouble : so will I hear thee and thou shalt praise Me." So help me, dear Lord, to do.

It is the work of the Holy Spirit " to take of the things of Christ and to show them unto us." It is He who brings us to the knowledge of Christ's power within us.

How real is Jesus to you in your daily life?

What is your response to bad news? Is it despair and fear? What do you say when you hear someone you love is very ill? Do you immediately realise that Jesus is in them? Do you say in your heart, " Jesus, Jesus, Jesus— " or do you begin to worry—as if God didn't exist?

He told us—" All power hath been given unto Me in Heaven and on earth." Do we believe it? Power over disease and death. Think of Him in the storm on the lake, " Why are ye fearful?"

We can learn to have that same ability to rely on the Father and know His peace—and, as Christians, we must never be satisfied till we have learned it. We do it in meditation.

LET MY FAITH BE QUICKENED BY THY HOLY SPIRIT WITHIN.

SILENCE

*Thanksgiving:* " O that men would therefore praise the Lord for His goodness and declare the wonders that He doeth for the children of men."

Thanks be to God.

---

## TRINITY XI

*Reading:* Romans 8$^{9\text{-}11}$.

*Prayer:* Grant that Thy power, Thy love and the mightiness of Thy Kingdom may be manifested through my life.

When we have trained ourselves to know that Jesus Christ is within us, by long persevering meditation, His presence becomes real to us and we learn to speak to Him and call upon Him many times during the day. Then we begin to know that His power is available to us in every need. If we cut ourselves or hurt ourselves in any way, we immediately know His presence and know His peace and healing power at work. Then we find that His power is infinite. The hurt heals very quickly : there are no bad after-effects. In times of danger we know His presence with us and it is sufficient for us—we are at peace.

The world puts limits to what is possible. It talks of evil as inevitable and of " incurable disease." It meets hatred with hatred. It does so because the world does not know God. He is not real to people who talk like that. They don't know Him. Do we? Not unless His reality becomes the possession of our whole mind and soul, and we learn this in meditation.

HOLY SPIRIT WITHIN, TEACH ME TO KNOW THE
LIVING CHRIST AND TO TRUST IN HIM.

*Thanksgiving:* Father, we thank Thee that Thou hast heard
us.

------

## TRINITY XII

*Reading:* 1 Chronicles $16^{23-25}$ and $^{28-29}$.

*Prayer:*   My soul doth magnify the Lord, and my spirit
hath rejoiced in God, my Saviour.

Our whole prayer life depends on what we believe about
God in the deepest part of our mind.  If we believe that
God is a great Being far away up in Heaven, our prayer
will be, " O Lord, hear our prayer and let our cry come
unto Thee."  If we believe that God is with us and in us, at
work, overcoming evil and working to perfect all things, we
will be silent in adoration and trust, knowing that all is
well.  " Your Father knoweth what ye have need of before
ye ask Him " (St. Matthew $6^8$).  If our ideas of God are
wrong, it leads to ineffective prayer.  Ye ask, and have not,
because ye ask amiss (James $4^3$).

Jesus made it very clear that God is always with us and
in us.  So, in meditation, we seek to know the truth about
God; to let God Himself teach us by waiting on Him.  He
then makes Himself known to us, not by talking to us
audibly, but by the growth of His Spirit of peace and love
and joy in our hearts.  So we come not only to know something about God, but to know Him in our own experience.

INFINITE SPIRIT OF LOVE I WOULD KNOW THEE
MORE DEEPLY.

*Thanksgiving:* O magnify the Lord our God and worship
Him : for the Lord our God is Holy.  Thanks be
to God.

# TRINITY XIII

*Reading:* St. John 5[17-21].

*Prayer:* Jesus, help me to follow Thy perfect human example that I may become like Thee in faith.

Jesus was very certain that His Father was always with Him and in Him. He knew that God was always at work, everywhere, in all the world. " My Father worketh."

That was the background to His simple faith. That was why He had no fear. He was surprised that His disciples feared. In the storm; Peter walking on the water; in the Upper Room; in face of death (Luke 8[50]).

" Fear not " was a frequent saying, and how we need to learn to trust like that.

God has made the world to express His own whole and perfect nature. He clothes the lilies and expresses something of His beauty in their beauty of colour and form and scent. How much more does He work in us to express Himself in us that we may be whole and holy as He is Himself.

And we are made in such a way that, when our minds are filled with the knowledge of His love and peace and goodness, the body naturally begins to express what the mind holds deeply. " This is life eternal that they may know the Father " (St. John 17[3]). How simple.

GIVE US KNOWLEDGE, DEAR LORD, KNOWLEDGE OF THYSELF.

SILENCE

*Thanksgiving:* Infinite love and peace and joy of God within : we adore and bless Thy Holy Name for ever.

---

# TRINITY XIV

*Reading:* St. John 15[4-11].

*Prayer:* Infinite spirit of God within, I adore Thee.

God is greater than the whole creation and yet also within. As a sponge, floating in the ocean, is surrounded by the water and is also filled with the water, and yet the sponge is not the water, so God is around us and in us and yet neither we nor creation are divine : creation is sacramental. " God is the Father who is above all and through all and in you all " (Eph. 4⁵).

The secret of life is to know this and so to abide in Him. " Abide in Me and I in you " (St. John 15⁴).

How do we do this? On the surface of our minds we move from one thought to another, and as we can only keep one thought in the conscious mind at a time, we can't be always thinking of God. Yet, underneath our consciousness there is an undercurrent of feeling, sometimes happy, sometimes not. If we are in love, we do our work and think of it, yet we have the undercurrent of joy in our loved ones. So we may abide in anxiety or fear or bitterness. In the same way we can learn to abide in God. We do it by learning to meditate. Then God is real to us always.

I AM WITH YOU ALWAYS, ABIDE IN ME.

SILENCE

*Thanksgiving:* I will give thanks unto Thee, O Lord, for Thou art ever with me : my strength and my salvation.

---

## TRINITY XV

*Reading:* St. Mark 7²⁰⁻²³.

*Prayer:* Like as the hart desireth the water brooks, so longeth my soul after Thee, O Lord.

To know that God is always with us, whether we are thinking of Him or not, is the secret of life. It can only come slowly as we persevere with meditation. Every time we meditate, we send down the truth into our deep mind and soul, and this truth gradually changes what is dark and negative in our mind. We are never conscious of this darkness but, ever since we were born, the world's way of thinking has been seeping into our unconscious mind. It is from this buried negative feeling that most disease and unhappiness comes. It is very necessary to change it and, as we dwell on the peace of God, His peace takes the place of fear and anxiety. His love takes the place of resentment, and so on.

But don't expect to be aware of this change while you are meditating. It is a very deep unconscious process, and so we don't look for the nice feelings or uplift while we meditate : we just say the words and let them work.

ABIDE IN ME AND KNOW MY LOVE WITHIN.

SILENCE

*Thanksgiving:* O give thanks unto the Lord and call upon Him. Tell the people what things He hath done.

---

## TRINITY XVI

*Reading:* Ecclesiasticus $3^{17-29}$.
*Prayer:* We thank Thee that Thou art ever with us and in us.

If we knew that this was really true, we would never worry or be anxious about anything, or even ever at a loss. We are self-conscious and feel inadequate, instead of being God-conscious. The world we live in is unaware of God, and its attitude has trained us to be the same. How common it is to hear people say, " Oh, dear, I feel frozen still with fear," or, " I'm sure I shall catch a chill standing in this cold wind." " I hope I won't catch a cold." Or, " I do feel so miserable, I just can't stand it any longer," or, " Well, after all, I can't help my feelings." Or someone we love is suddenly ill and we say : " Isn't it ghastly, the doctor says he can't possibly get better."

Where do these feelings, these negative ideas come from? They come from our past training, from our deep mind. It has not been made new or redeemed, or healed by Christ, as yet. But it can be, through meditation. There is no need for us to be the slave of our deeply buried thoughts and assumptions. We need not go on being worldly in this way.

I AM WITH YOU, BEHOLD I MAKE ALL THINGS NEW.

SILENCE

*Thanksgiving:* Great and marvellous are Thy works, Lord God almighty, Thou King of Saints. We glorify Thy Name, for Thou only art Holy.

---

## TRINITY XVII

*Reading:* Romans 8$^{21\text{-}24}$.

*Prayer:* Grant us, dear Lord, a deeper sense of the evil of the world in which we are involved and a deeper penitence for it.

God has made us: why then do we need to be made new? Because we are not what God wants us to be. Evil has spoiled the whole creation and us. St. Paul reminds us that the whole creation groans and travails in pain (Rom. 8$^{22}$). Creation has fallen short of God's purpose of expressing and reflecting His own perfection, as well as the human race. We were made to manifest God's glory: and we don't. Our negative thoughts—thoughts of hatred, lust, jealousy, greed, self—and our doubts and fears are evidence of how unlike God we have become and of our need for cleansing, healing, forgiving, that we may become sons of God, manifesting His glory, His love and joy and peace and goodness. We need to be purified and made new. We are involved in the evil of the world: dark terrible evil, and it is deep within us now.

FATHER, FORGIVE, AND TEACH US TO FORGIVE.

SILENCE

*Thanksgiving:* Father, we thank Thee that Thy love is overcoming all evil. We praise and bless Thee.

57

*Reading:* Psalm 62$^{1-2, 5-8, 11-12}$.

*Prayer:*    O Lord our God, show the light of Thy countenance and we shall be whole.

God is always at work in us, wanting to enable us to become His true sons and daughters and to grow into His likeness. So in meditation we wait on Him : for in Him is all that we need.

" He verily is my strength and my salvation " (i.e. health).

" He is my defence."

" In God is my health and my glory."

" Power belongeth unto God." And power is not force : it is adequacy—it is all that we need.

And His strength is never passive : it is at work in all the world; every bud opens by His power alone. So, in all the circumstances of life, God is there in them, and always adequate to our need, if we only know it. The circumstances may be difficult——a broken marriage—a quarrel—one whom we love is ill. But that is not the whole picture : God is real and He is present, and nothing can separate us from the love of God. All is well, all is well, and again, all is well.

THAT I MAY ENTER NOW INTO THE KNOWLEDGE
OF THY POWER WITHIN ME.

### SILENCE

*Thanksgiving:* And now, Father, we thank Thee that Thou hast heard us and we know that Thou hearest us always. Therefore we praise Thee for ever.

---

## TRINITY XIX

*Reading:* Jeremiah 9$^{23-24}$.

*Prayer:*    Help us to take heed unto that light which shineth in a dark place until the day dawns and the day star arises in our hearts.

Think of God's adequacy again. " The Lord is my

Shepherd, therefore can I lack nothing." "Son, thou art ever with Me, all that I have is thine " (St. Luke 15³¹).

What is it that God has, which is now within us, waiting to come out into expression and so to make us true sons of God?

Think of God as He is shown to us in Jesus: His deep love—" I have not called you servants, I have called you friends " (St. John 15¹⁵).

His compassion: His quick response to need: " I will come and heal him " (St. Matthew 8⁷), to the widow of Nain and to Jairus (St. Luke 8⁵⁰).

His courtesy and tenderness: the woman taken in adultery (St. John 8³); the Woman of Samaria (St. John 4¹⁰).

His calmness in danger: in the boat in the storm (St. Mark 4³⁹).

There was true humanity adding the beauty of gracefulness to every action and, in that, revealing God: and, " all that I have is thine."

WAIT ON ME, FOR ALL THAT I HAVE IS THINE.

SILENCE

*Thanksgiving:* The Lord shall be thine everlasting light. Thanks be to God.

---

TRINITY XX

*Reading:* Revelation 11¹⁵.

*Prayer:*  Great and marvellous are Thy works, Lord God Almighty, just and true are Thy ways, Thou King of Saints. Who shall not love Thee, O Lord, and glorify Thy name, for Thou only art holy.

We can only give out what we have received and known. " Out of the abundance of the heart, the mouth speaketh." It is also true that what we *are* speaks far louder to others than any of our words. God's gracefulness can only be seen in us if we learn to wait on Him. It is not what we do ourselves in meditation which helps us, but what we wait on God to do in us. As we practise meditation every day of our lives, learning to let go and let God make Himself known to us, we begin to find that the words are less important: God is very real and we do not think it waste of time to be still in His presence: we are sure that He speaks and so we wait for Him. Gradually He changes us and renews our character. The sinful, ugly side of our nature is changed, and humbly we thank Him. "For it doth not yet appear what we shall be."

I WILL WAIT ON THEE, DEAR LORD, THAT I MAY BE MADE NEW.

*Thanksgiving:* We give Thee thanks, O Lord God Almighty, which art and wast and art to come.

---

## TRINITY XXI

*Reading:* St. John 5$^{24-29}$ and $^{40}$.

*Prayer:* The voice of joy and health is in the dwelling of the righteous: the right hand of the Lord bringeth mighty things to pass. I shall not die but live and show forth the glory of the Lord. Thanks be to God.

When Jesus spoke of death, He often meant the death of living as if God didn't exist. Life as so many people are content to live it, is not life at all, it is death. "In the midst of life we are in death." Is that what makes life so unsatisfying to many people?

God can be all round us and in us and yet we may be blind to Him. He was in the world, and the world was made by Him, but the world knew Him not (St. John 1$^{10}$). But to know Him and to believe in Him is to enter into life —that is, into real personal experience of knowing the power of God's life in our daily life so that we find our faith growing more simple, our trust in God stronger, our calmness in face of difficulties greater, and a deeper sense of joy growing in our hearts, and, besides this, an experience of greater physical well-being, so that we have a greater resistance to illness and less expectation of ill health and other troubles : for God is with us, and He is life within us.

QUICKEN THE POWER OF THY LIFE WITHIN ME THAT I MAY LIVE TO THY GLORY.

SILENCE

*Thanksgiving:* O praise the Lord, for it is a good thing to praise the Lord; yea, a joyful thing it is to be thankful.

---

# TRINITY XXII

*Reading:* Proverbs 4$^{20-22}$.

*Prayer:* My soul truly waiteth still upon God, for of Him cometh my salvation. In God is my health and my glory, and in God is my strength.

The Christ whose life is always in us is not a stained-glass window figure—not "gentle Jesus, meek and mild." He is Creator of the world; the Messiah; it is He who gives purpose to the whole world, for He is the leader to the Kingdom of God on earth who calls us into fellowship with Himself, that with all other members of the Community which is His Body, the Church, we may challenge the evil of the world and overcome it. The work He calls us to, cannot be done by individuals alone; it needs a community in action, and that is what the Church is meant to be. But it must know that the power that enables it to be Christ in the world comes from His life within every member of His Body.

I WOULD BE ALIVE WITH THY LIFE WITHIN.

SILENCE

*Thanksgiving:* Praise the Lord for He is gracious. O sing
praises unto His name for it is lovely. We will
give thanks to Him for He hath heard us.

## TRINITY XXIII

*Reading:* Romans 12$^{3-5}$.

*Prayer:* Help me, dear Lord, to know my unity with all
those who suffer in Thee, and grant me a share
in Thy compassion and hope for their wholeness.

The purpose of meditation is always, firstly that we may
learn to know God more deeply and have fellowship with
Him; secondly, that we may become better fitted as members
of His Body, His Church, to serve Him. It can also be used
to help other people who are in need or in sickness. Their
real need is a deeper knowledge of God's reality, of His love
and peace, of His will to heal and of His power to do so.

It is possible to share our knowledge of this kind with
those for whom we meditate, because there is a very real
unity between members of the Body of Christ: and mind
touches mind on the deepest level of the unconscious mind
and soul. If, with someone else " in mind," we enter into a
deep consciousness of God's peace, that consciousness will be
shared. We do not try to exert any influence ourselves, nor
do we try to push anything into the other person, nor do
we use our will or even try to put anything into his mind.
We wait on God in Christ, allowing His peace to fill our
minds, knowing that the other person will also experience
God's peace, which is his great need. Think now of someone you know who is ill or in trouble. Thank God that in
Christ you and he are one—then meditate.

I WILL BE STILL AND TAKE HOLD OF THY PEACE.

SILENCE

*Thanksgiving:* Father, we thank Thee for Thy peace, which
is strength and wholeness to us both.

# TRINITY XXIV

*Reading:* 1 John 1$^{5-7}$.

*Prayer:*  Let Thy perfect beauty and goodness come forth, dear Lord, that we may glorify Thee.

God is eternal goodness. Are we certain of this? We need to know it very deeply in our minds if we are going to meet the evil of the world and not to be overcome by it. So many people attribute evil to God, which is blasphemy, because God is light and in Him is no darkness at all. (1 John 1$^5$). How often we hear—" Why has this been sent to me?" The ideas—that God sends sickness, that it is His will or punishment, that He is far away up in Heaven, that when a child dies of sickness it is because God wants him in Heaven—are very common still.

When you or a friend are very ill, do you worry? When in danger, do you fear?

Yet the truth is that God is eternal goodness and He never changes. He is always with us and always at work, and as goodness is the very essence of His nature He works to express it in all the world.

Negative and wrong ideas of God come from the thought and unbelief of the world, and this sinks into our deep minds. We must counteract and overcome this with the Truth.

I AM ETERNAL GOODNESS WITHIN YOU. TRUST IN ME.

### SILENCE

*Thanksgiving:* Quicken Thou the knowledge of Thy goodness within me and give me a thankful heart. Thanks be to God.

# THE SUNDAY NEXT BEFORE ADVENT

*Reading:* Revelation 3$^{14-22}$.

*Prayer:*    Make me a clean heart, O Lord, and renew a right spirit within me.

This is the last Sunday of the Church's year and next Sunday is Advent—new year's day for Church people. So we look back in penitence. How much more we could have done for Christ's cause and how much more whole we should be. Why is it that so often it is people who are not Christians who are most active in opposing evil and striving for a cleaner, juster world? It is high time to awake out of sleep and to amend our ways. Repentance for our sins and failures is not enough if we stop at being sorry and confessing our sins; we need to amend and to be re-made in our deepest consciousness. Out of the heart proceed adulteries, covetousness, pride, evil thoughts, foolishness—yes, and laziness and self-concern and lack of love. We are not healed of these till our whole deep consciousness has been re-made in prayer and meditation, which reaches deep down to the heart and soul. We need a new relationship to God, acceptance of forgiveness and a deeper love which makes us devoted sons of God, giving ourselves to His Cause.

LET THY FORGIVENESS, DEAR LORD, BE TO ME HEALING AND WHOLENESS.

### SILENCE

*Thanksgiving:* Lord Jesus, our Leader, we give ourselves to Thee for the cause of Thy glorious Kingdom, for joy or for sorrow, for success or for failure, for life or for death, now and for evermore.   Amen.